Life on the Homefront during the American Revolution

Helen Mason

CRABTREE
Publishing Company
www.crabtreebooks.com

Understanding The American Revolution

Author: Helen Mason
Publishing plan research and development:
Sean Charlebois, Reagan Miller
Crabtree Publishing Company
Editors: Leslie Jenkins, Janet Sweet, Lynn Peppas
Proofreaders: Lisa Slone, Kelly McNiven
Editorial director: Kathy Middleton
Production coordinator: Shivi Sharma
Creative director: Amir Abbasi
Cover design: Samara Parent and Margaret Salter
Photo research: Nivisha Sinha
Maps: Paul Brinkdopke
Production coordinator and prepress technician: Samara Parent
Print coordinator: Katherine Berti

Written, developed, and produced by Planman Technologies

Cover: *Mrs. Murray's Strategy* by E. Percy Moran. Mrs. Mary Murray was said to have entertained British officers in order to delay them so that George Washington's troops could retreat from New York without capture.

Title page: (main) A 19th century cotton plantation on the Mississippi River.
(bottom) American heroine Molly Pitcher helps fight the British at the Battle of Monmouth in 1778.

Photographs and Reproductions
Front Cover: Library of Congress (b) / Shutterstock (t); Title Page: ©Archive Images / Alamy / IndiaPicture; ©Ivy Close Images / Alamy / IndiaPicture; Table of Content: Christoff / Shutterstock; Library of Congress; Library of Congress; Library of Congress; Universal / IndiaPicture; Kean Collection / Archive Photos / Getty Images; Introduction: ©Jeff Greenberg / Alamy / IndiaPicture; Chapter 1: ©Jeff Greenberg / Alamy / IndiaPicture; Chapter 2: ©Jeff Greenberg / Alamy / IndiaPicture; Chapter 3: ©Jeff Greenberg / Alamy / IndiaPicture; Chapter 4: ©Jeff Greenberg / Alamy / IndiaPicture; Chapter 5: ©Jeff Greenberg / Alamy / IndiaPicture; Page 5: Christoff / Shutterstock; Page 9: Library of Congress; Page 11: ©Jeff Greenberg / Alamy / IndiaPicture (t); ©Archive Images / Alamy / IndiaPicture (c); Library of Congress (b); Page 12: Madeleine Openshaw / Shutterstock (l); Universal / IndiaPicture (b); Page 13: Library of Congress; Page 16: Library of Congress; Page 17: Library of Congress (r); Library of Congress (b); Page 18: Library of Congress; Page 21: Library of Congress; Page 24: Library of Congress; Page 26: Hulton Archive / Getty Images; Page 27: Library of Congress; Page 28: Library of Congress; Page 30: Library of Congress; Page 31: Library of Congress; Page 35: Universal / IndiaPicture; Page 37: ©dbimages / Alamy / IndiaPicture; Page 39: Kean Collection / Archive Photos / Getty Images;
(t = top, b = bottom, l = left, c = center, r = right, bkgd = background, fgd = foreground)

Library and Archives Canada Cataloguing in Publication

Mason, Helen, 1950-
Life on the homefront during the American Revolution / Helen Mason.

(Understanding the American Revolution)
Includes bibliographical references and index.
Issued also in electronic format.
ISBN 978-0-7787-0801-8 (bound).--ISBN 978-0-7787-0812-4 (pbk.)

1. United States--History--Revolution, 1775-1783--Social aspects--Juvenile literature. 2. Women--United States--Social conditions--18th century--Juvenile literature. 3. African Americans--Social conditions--18th century--Juvenile literature. I. Title. II. Series: Understanding the American Revolution (St. Catharines, Ont.)

E209.M27 2013   j973.3'1   C2013-900238-3

Library of Congress Cataloging-in-Publication Data

CIP available at Library of Congress

Crabtree Publishing Company
www.crabtreebooks.com   1-800-387-7650

Printed in Canada/022013/BF20130114

Published in Canada
Crabtree Publishing
616 Welland Ave.
St. Catharines, Ontario
L2M 5V6

Published in the United States
Crabtree Publishing
PMB 59051
350 Fifth Avenue, 59th Floor
New York, New York 10118

Published in the United Kingdom
Crabtree Publishing
Maritime House
Basin Road North, Hove
BN41 1WR

Published in Australia
Crabtree Publishing
3 Charles Street
Coburg North
VIC 3058

TABLE of CONTENTS

Introduction

The story of the young American colonies is full of both struggle and hope. During the American Revolution, the soldiers were not the only ones affected. The war also came to the homefront, or the everyday places where everyday people supported the war.

Major Events

1607–1732
The 13 colonies are founded in America

1754–1763
Great Britain defeats France in the French and Indian War

1764
April 15
Parliament passes the Sugar Act

1765
March 22
Parliament passes the Stamp Act

March 24
Parliament passes the Quartering Act

1766
March
Parliament **repeals** the Stamp Act but passes the Declaratory Act

A New Land

The American colonists and their ancestors traveled from Great Britain across the Atlantic Ocean to start new lives in a rugged new country. Without a doubt, life was hard on the colonial **frontier**. But the promise of opportunity, **prosperity**, and liberty was a powerful attraction for many. With hard work, courage, and determination, the colonists could tap into America's rich natural resources. They could create their own livelihood, build their own **economy**, and set down roots.

When the American Revolution broke out, these ordinary citizens supported the war effort by maintaining law and order, supplying the army with **goods**, and keeping up farms and businesses. These efforts were a major part of the **Patriots**' victory in the war. Instead of being on the battle front, everyday people struggled for the Patriot cause on the homefront.

Great Britain's Early Colonies

As the head of the British Empire, Great Britain **prospered** from the colonies in America. The colonies provided Britain with natural resources and valuable goods such as food, tobacco, lumber, furs, and rum. The colonies bought finished goods from Britain. Britain also provided protection and an established system of government to the colonies.

The Colonies' Relationship with Britain Sours

The British government needed new sources of **revenue** to pay off its debts from the French and Indian War. Parliament voted to increase tax revenue from the colonies in acts such as the Stamp Act of 1765. Parliament believed it was fair for the colonies to pay a share of the costs, since they were part of the Empire.

Patriotism and War

The colonists were far away from Britain and had been fending for themselves for nearly two generations.

Many colonists argued that Parliament had no right to tax them because the colonies were not directly represented in Parliament. Angered by increasing taxes, many colonists decided to follow Patriot leaders who were calling for independence. In 1775, the colonists armed themselves in a war against Great Britain.

After the War

After the war ended and the Treaty of Paris was signed, everyone had to get along. Some people left America, either by choice or by need. Others stayed to embrace democracy and to help the homefront grow into a new nation known as the United States of America.

The Revolutionary flag

Major Events

1767

June 29
Parliament passes the Townshend Revenue Act

1768

June 10
The British seize John Hancock's ship, the *Liberty*

1770

March 5
The Boston Massacre

1773

May 10
Parliament passes the Tea Act

December 16
The Boston Tea Party

1774

March
Parliament passes the Intolerable Acts

September 5
First Continental Congress begins to meet

1775

April 15
Revolutionary War begins between the colonies and Britain

1776

July 4
The Declaration of Independence is signed

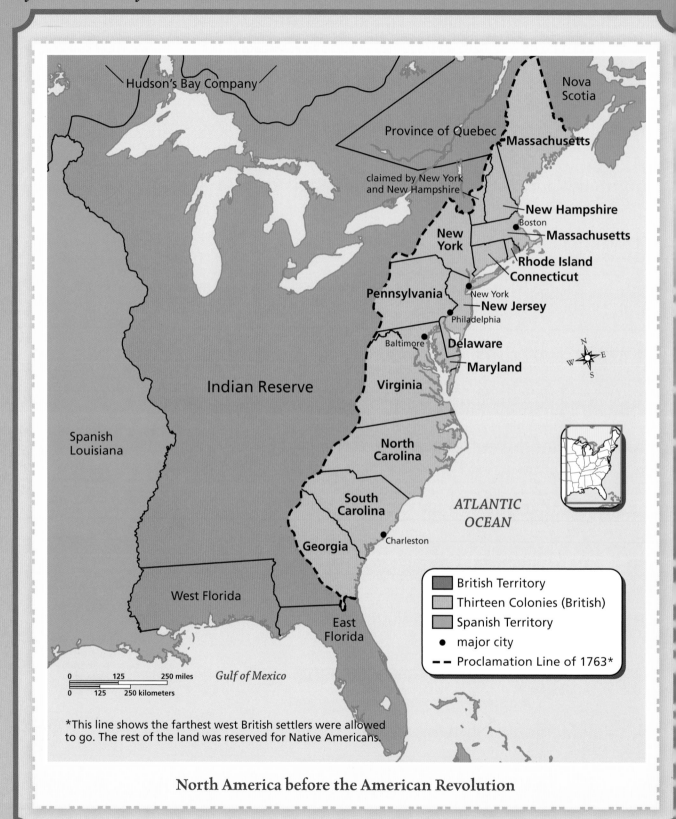

Hudson's Bay Company

Nova Scotia

Province of Quebec

Massachusetts

claimed by New York and New Hampshire

New Hampshire

Boston

New York

Massachusetts

Rhode Island
Connecticut

Pennsylvania

New York

New Jersey

Philadelphia

Baltimore

Delaware

Maryland

Indian Reserve

Virginia

Spanish Louisiana

North Carolina

South Carolina

Charleston

ATLANTIC OCEAN

Georgia

West Florida

East Florida

Gulf of Mexico

	British Territory
	Thirteen Colonies (British)
	Spanish Territory
●	major city
– – –	Proclamation Line of 1763*

0 125 250 miles
0 125 250 kilometers

*This line shows the farthest west British settlers were allowed to go. The rest of the land was reserved for Native Americans.

North America before the American Revolution

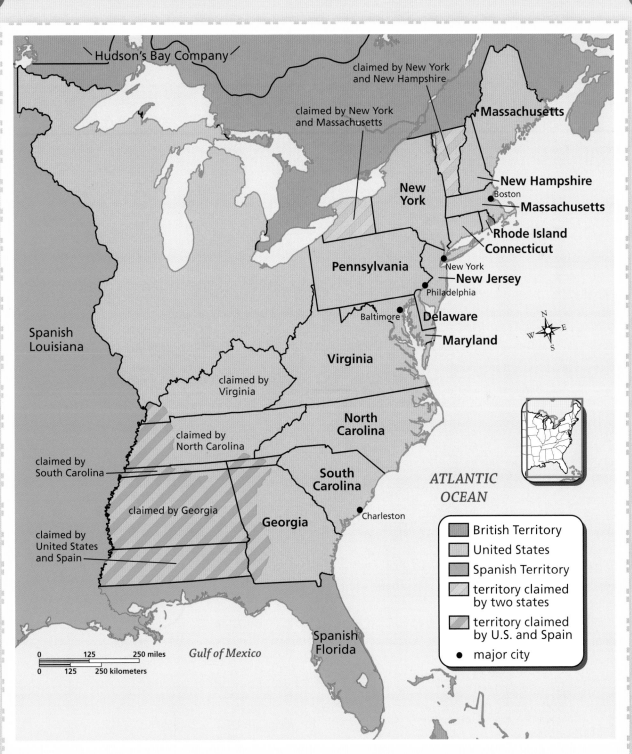

The United States after the American Revolution

1 Daily Life in Colonial America

During the American Revolution, many colonists left their families to join the fight. The men, women, and children who remained on the homefront faced times of hardship as America plunged into war.

A World Turned Upside Down

Wars do not only affect the soldiers fighting in them. During the Revolutionary War, colonial families found their world turned upside down.

A Struggling Economy

The British army occupied buildings, preventing colonists from building businesses or collecting rent. When the British closed Boston Harbor in 1774, many colonists could not do their jobs and earn money. British navy blockades nearly eliminated the fishing industry in the Northern colonies, and cut off the supply of European goods.

Battles on Doorsteps

Revolutionary battles sometimes came to the colonists' front doorsteps. Fights broke out in village town squares and on roads connecting farms to towns. It was not a very safe time to travel.

> *Here once the embattled farmers stood and fired the shot heard round the world.*
>
> —Ralph Waldo Emerson, 1837

Farming Life of Colonial People

In colonial America, everyone had to work hard in order to survive. Most colonists survived by farming. Colonial men had to cut down huge trees to clear fields for growing food. Nothing was wasted. The wood was used to build their houses and whatever was left was burned to cook meals and keep the house warm.

In the spring, the fields were planted with crops. During the summer, they tended the crops, and in the fall it was time for the harvest. The whole family picked the crops to store for the winter months ahead. In addition to farming, colonial men cared for their animals, made shoes, repaired the house and barn, and made toys for their children.

Hunting for Food

Hunting and fishing were necessities for survival on the homefront. Colonial men hunted for wild birds and animals. If harsh weather ruined their crops, wild **game** was sometimes the only food available to eat. Hunters caught and ate birds, wild turkeys, bears, lynx, wolves, elk, deer, raccoons, beavers, and squirrels. They used the hides and furs for clothing.

What Do You Know!

WORKING WITH THEIR HANDS

In order to survive, colonists had to learn many skills. They needed to be able to shoot a gun and use an ax. They made farm equipment and furniture out of wood. Some farmers learned other trades, such as blacksmithing. Farmers could earn extra money doing jobs like these for their neighbors.

Farming in colonial America took a large effort. Some wealthy families owned slaves to work their fields and care for their animals.

What Do You Know!

MAKING LINEN

Colonial women were responsible for making their families' clothes, often out of linen. Linen is a fabric made from the flax plant. About 2 acres (0.8 hectares) of flax were typically needed to make enough clothes for a family. Flax was planted in early spring and harvested in July. It was bundled and dried, and the fibers had to be separated.

To make cloth, the longer fibers were removed and spun into thread while wet. This flax thread was then woven into cloth. A popular cloth called **linsey-woolsey** was made by alternating threads of wool and linen. The material was inexpensive and lasted a long time, but it was very scratchy.

A Woman's Work Was Never Done

Colonial women worked just as hard as the men. Everything that the family ate and wore depended on them. When sheep were sheared, women cleaned and **carded** wool, spun yarn, and then wove fabric. The fabric was used to make clothes for the family.

On the homefront, colonial women spent most of the day cooking. All of the cooking and baking for the family was done over an open fire.

Colonial women also took care of the animals, preserved meat, and dried food. They made most of the things that would be bought in a grocery store today, such as soap, candles, some medicines, and many toys. They did all of this on top of caring for the children. Colonial women usually had large families, with most women having a baby every two years. .

As well as their home chores, some women worked as **midwives**, **merchants**, printers, and even doctors. If the husband got sick or died—or went to war—his wife took on his work as well as her own.

> " *He that will not work shall not eat.* "
> —John Smith, Virginia, 1608

Life in the Southern Colonies

Colonial families in the South often lived on large farms or **plantations**. A plantation was similar to a small village. It included a large house or mansion, with the kitchen in a separate building. A plantation could also have a dairy, a smokehouse, a blacksmith shop, a carpentry shop, stables, and a separate area with small cabins for **slaves**. Both the owners and the slaves had to work hard to keep the plantation running. The owners were often very wealthy and could afford luxuries, such as fine furniture and fancy clothes imported from Europe.

Colonial Social Classes

Colonial society was divided into various social classes.

GENTRY The gentry included large landowners, very wealthy merchants, and **financiers**. The gentry had large amounts of land, and many owned slaves. Many of the generals and **statesmen** during the American Revolution came from this class.

MIDDLING The middling group included tradespeople, meaning a person who had a special skill. Many were storeowners, who depended on trade with Britain. The middling class also included professionals, such as lawyers and doctors.

FARMERS Most colonists belonged to this group and lived on farms or in small towns. A farm usually consisted of a husband, wife, and children, and sometimes included a slave or hired hand.

INDENTURED SERVANTS An **indentured servant** was a person who agreed to work for a set period of time, usually seven years, for someone. In return, they received money and a place to live. Their master often paid for their trip to America as part of the indenture.

FREE BLACKS This group included black men from Northern colonies who had been freed or whose ancestors had been freed from slavery. It was difficult to be a free black during the Revolution because much of society did not accept free blacks.

SLAVES In 1760, almost 20 percent of the colonies' population consisted of slaves. There were three divisions of slaves:
- Some slaves worked in the fields to plant, tend, and pick crops like tobacco and cotton;
- More skilled slaves cooked, did laundry, performed household chores, or were carpenters, blacksmiths, or **coopers**;
- Slaves with the highest status lived in New England and the Middle Colonies. These slaves worked as household servants and craftsmen. Some were even taught how to read and write.

Gentry

Southern gentry

↓

Middling

↓

Farmers

Farmers

↓

Indentured Servants

↓

Free Blacks

↓

Slaves

A slave auction

A Jacob's ladder is made from blocks of wood held together with string or ribbons; the toy is easy to make and fun to play with.

Colonial Children

Life on the homefront for children was busy and full of hard work. Children started doing chores at a very young age. Boys worked with their fathers in the fields helping with the planting and weeding. They also cared for animals and hunted for food. As they grew up, they often trained in their fathers' trade.

Like the boys, colonial girls worked hard, except that they helped with inside chores. Girls took care of the younger children, fed the chickens, collected the eggs, milked the cows, made butter and cheese, and helped in the garden. As they got older, they learned spinning, sewing, and other skills they would need to start their own families.

For fun, children sometimes played board or card games, or with homemade toys like a Jacob's ladder. In some colonies, boisterous games like tag and hide-and-seek were **banned**.

School Days

Some children were lucky enough to attend **dame schools** which were taught by a female neighbor. The teacher often did her household chores while she taught children their letters, simple words, and how to count.

In New England, village boys might go to a **grammar school** where they learned Latin, math, and other subjects. In the Southern Colonies, all young children—both boys and girls—were taught at home by their parents or a private tutor. Teenage boys from wealthy families might go to college. At this time, girls did not go to college, instead becoming wives and mothers.

Young children went to a dame school, where a neighbor woman taught the alphabet, counting, and simple prayers.

The Revolution Changed Lives

Before the American Revolution, people in the colonies supported each other, shared similar beliefs, and helped each other build barns and houses. They pitched in during emergencies. When someone was sick, neighbors stepped in to care for children and feed livestock.

War Changed Attitudes

The American Revolution dramatically changed the lives of the colonists. Communities split down **Loyalist** and Patriot lines. Instead of working together, some families and neighbors now fought on different sides of the conflict. Peoples' homes and farms were no longer safe. Some were taken over as soldiers' quarters and some were burned by neighbors who supported the opposing side of the war.

Sometimes, the use of churches, schools, and meeting halls also changed. One church was used to house cavalry horses. Schools and meeting halls were used as hospitals or even prisons to hold people who were against the **occupying army**.

> *We must all hang together, or assuredly we shall all hang separately.*
>
> —Benjamin Franklin, 1776

Colonists worked together to build houses and barns.

The Patriots Challenge the Loyalists

During the American Revolution, the colonists were divided. Some were Loyalists supporting Great Britain. Some were Patriots supporting an independent America.

Important Decisions

For colonists, deciding which side to support was a difficult decision. The Patriots had new ideas about how America should be governed. Many well-spoken Patriots, such as Thomas Jefferson, Samuel Adams, John Adams, Patrick Henry, Thomas Paine, and George Washington, urged the colonists to consider America as an independent nation. These influential men later became important leaders of America.

But it could be risky to switch loyalties from Britain to the Patriots. American colonists benefited from trade with Britain, which was one of the most powerful nations in the world at that time. Britain also had an established government that provided resources, policies, protection, and other important support to the 13 colonies. Only after the British Parliament demanded the colonists pay increasing taxes—without listening to their concerns—did the Patriots receive wide support from many colonists.

> *These are the times that try men's souls.*
>
> —Thomas Paine, December 23, 1776

Who Can Tax Us?

One of the main disagreements between Great Britain and America was over taxes. Fighting the French and Indian War had cost a lot of money. Britain thought that Americans should help to pay the war's debts, since the war was fought in America.

Britain Imposes Taxes

Between 1764 and 1765, the British government tried to raise money by charging new taxes:

- The 1764 Sugar Act charged a tax on molasses and sugar, which the colonists used to make rum.
- The 1765 Stamp Act demanded the colonists to buy tax stamps for all printed documents, such as newspapers, legal papers, and marriage licenses.
- The 1765 Quartering Act required the colonists to provide housing, food, and ammunition to British troops and officials upholding British rule in America.

Colonists Respond with Anger

These acts angered many colonists for several reasons. They did not believe Britain had the right to force Americans to pay taxes. They believed that any new taxes should be decided by the colonists themselves. They also resented the large numbers of British troops being sent to America. They saw the military presence as an attempt to clamp down on the colonists' freedoms.

After the Sugar Act, angry Boston merchants stopped buying British goods containing sugar. They hoped that this action would make Parliament think twice about the tax. Representatives from nine colonies signed a petition to have the Stamp Act repealed.

Speaking out against Parliament inspired many groups of Patriots to take action. Calling themselves the "Sons of Liberty," one group of Patriots ganged up on the British agents sent from Britain to collect the stamp tax. An early idea of independence was beginning to grow.

Major Events

1770

March 5
Boston Massacre

1773

May 10
Parliament passes the Tea Act

December 16
Patriots respond to the Tea Act with the Boston Tea Party

1774

March
Parliament passes the Intolerable Acts

September
First Continental Congress begins

1775

April 19
British and Patriots clash during the Battles of Lexington and Concord

August 23
King George III declares the colonies in open rebellion

The British Response

The British Parliament did listen to some of the protests. In 1766, it replaced the Sugar Act with another act that reduced the tax. Parliament also repealed the Stamp Act. But Parliament also passed an act saying that the British government had a right to pass laws ruling the colonies. Hostilities cooled down for the time being.

The Townshend Revenue Act

By 1767, Parliament wanted to raise taxes again. This time they charged taxes on glass, paint, oil, lead, paper, and tea. The money raised from these taxes would pay for British governors, judges, and **customs** officers. It would also pay for a British army in America.

Patriot Reactions

The Townshend Act inflamed the Patriots. They refused to buy the taxed products. Trade with Great Britain fell off by 50 percent. In Boston, officials who tried to collect the duties were mobbed. Two British regiments were called in to maintain peace. This sparked further violence between the British army and the Patriots.

 Patriot Ideas

- Everyone has rights that the government cannot take away, such as the right to property. Taxation takes away some rightful property.
- Representation in Parliament would not be practical, and without representation, taxation is unfair.
- The colonists can govern themselves.
- The colonies did their part in the French and Indian War by fighting. They shouldn't have to pay for it, too.
- The British troops are a threat to colonists' safety and freedom.
- Britain is only trying to take advantage of the colonies and colonists.

 Loyalist Ideas

- A strong empire is best for all.
- Everyone profits from trade with Great Britain. **Boycotts** hurt the colonists, too.
- Colonists are British subjects and must obey the laws, just like people in Great Britain.
- The colonies should help pay debts from the French and Indian War since it was fought to defend them.
- The colonies could not defend themselves without Britain's military.
- British government and military are necessary to keep the peace.

People at the Time

John Adams

John Adams was a lawyer and Patriot who wrote against the Stamp Act. He was elected to the Massachusetts Assembly in 1770. He was also one of five Massachusetts representatives at the First Continental Congress and a strong supporter of independence. Adams became the first vice president under George Washington. He served as the nation's second president from 1787 to 1801.

American Ship Seized

In 1768 the *Liberty*, an American ship belonging to John Hancock, arrived in Boston. The crew tried to avoid paying the taxes on the goods on board, but more customs officers arrived to enforce the law. Tempers flared, and a mob formed. They attacked the officers, setting one of their boats on fire. John Hancock was later charged with smuggling. He was known to be guilty. However, he was defended by his cousin, John Adams, and was **acquitted**.

The Boston Massacre

Late in the afternoon of March 5, 1770, an angry group of Patriots taunted the British soldiers guarding the Boston Customs House. One member threw a club, knocking down a British soldier. In response, another soldier fired into the crowd.

The mob attacked. In the fight, five Patriots were killed. The British soldiers were arrested and tried for murder. Most were acquitted because they had been defending themselves. Later, the British removed the taxes they had imposed on everything except tea. American merchants began importing British goods again, but bad feelings continued.

People at the Time

Samuel Adams

Samuel Adams was one of the first people to argue for independence from Britain. He sent many letters to newspapers and business leaders. He signed the letters with different names so that it seemed like many people supported independence. In addition to protesting the Stamp Act, Adams also helped to organize the Boston Tea Party.

Crispus Attucks, a former slave, was the first person killed during the Boston Massacre. His death inflamed Patriot tempers.

The Tea Act and the Boston Tea Party

In 1773, Parliament passed the Tea Act. This act created a **monopoly**, meaning that colonists could buy tea only from the British East India Company. In response, the colonists boycotted all British goods. In December, a group of Patriots from the Sons of Liberty disguised themselves as Native Americans. They boarded the East India Company ships that were anchored in Boston Harbor, and threw the entire cargo of tea overboard as an act of protest.

The British Retaliated

In 1774, responding to the Boston Tea Party, the British passed four acts that became known as the Intolerable Acts. Under these acts, the British clamped down further on the colony of Massachusetts. They closed the port of Boston as punishment for the Boston Tea Party. This crippled Boston merchants' ability to make a living. The Intolerable Acts also allowed British officials who had been accused of crimes to be tried in Britain, far away from their accusers. And they required colonists to house British soldiers in their homes.

The First Continental Congress

In September, the legislatures of 12 colonies sent representatives to Philadelphia for the first Continental Congress. Georgia did not attend. Initially, the representatives did not want independence. They wanted Britain to repeal the Intolerable Acts. They agreed to boycott British goods if the acts were not repealed by December 1, 1774. If nothing was done by September 10, 1775, they would also stop sending goods to Great Britain. Members also signed a petition to King George III. They voted to meet again on May 10, 1775. King George III was unwilling to listen and on August 23, 1775, he declared the colonies in open rebellion.

> " *The die is now cast. The Colonies must either submit or triumph.*
>
> —King George III, 1774 "

People during the War

General Thomas Gage

From 1763 to 1775, General Gage commanded the British forces in North America. He was appointed military governor of Massachusetts in 1774. General Gage advised Parliament that a decision to repeal the Intolerable Acts would satisfy many colonists. He also reported that it would take a large army to defeat the Americans.

What Happened to the Loyalists?

A large number of Loyalists lived in New York, Pennsylvania, and New Jersey. During the war, the colonial governments passed laws against Loyalists. In many cases, their property was **confiscated** or heavily taxed. Many Loyalists' homes were burned and their possessions were stolen. Others were attacked and some killed. George Washington considered the Loyalists to be **traitors**. He and other Patriots treated Loyalists as enemies. Even those who did not fight for the British were treated badly.

Beginning in 1776, more than 100,000 Loyalists fled the 13 colonies. This number included white settlers, blacks, and some Native Americans. The greatest number moved to Canada, where they were called United Empire Loyalists. The Loyalists played a large role in Canadian history. After the war, others **migrated** to Great Britain or the Caribbean islands. Slaves who fought for Great Britain were promised freedom. When they migrated, they were freed. Many black Loyalists who remained in the United States were denied their freedom and forced back into slavery.

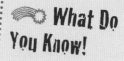

What Do You Know!

NATIVE AMERICAN LOYALIST
Joseph Brant was a Mohawk chief and British Loyalist. After the American Revolution, he and his followers moved to Canada. There they received a land grant from the British and settled in what is now southern Ontario. Brant spent the last years of his life translating the Bible into Mohawk.

> *Better to live under one tyrant a thousand miles away, than a thousand tyrants one mile away.*
>
> —Daniel Bliss, Loyalist from Massachusetts Bliss who fled to Canada and became a chief justice

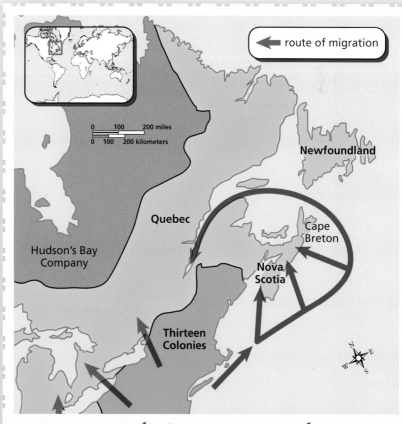

Loyalist Movement to Canada

Women Join the Fight

Major Events

1774

October
North Carolina women boycott British goods during the Edenton Tea Party

1775

September
Deborah Champion delivers money and papers to General Washington

1776

March
Abigail Adams writes asking John Adams to consider women in the new constitution

November
Margaret Corbin fights against the British

1777

October
Anna Maria Lane wounded at Battle of Germantown

December 3
Lydia Darragh sends information about British attack plans

The Revolutionary War involved all people in the colonies. Women fought hard for independence by supporting the troops from home and by being on the front lines as spies and soldiers.

Women and the War Effort

During the American Revolution, women proved themselves "the best Patriots America can boast," as George Washington wrote. When their men went off to fight, women continued with their usual jobs. They also stepped in to do the men's work. Colonial women usually raised children, grew food, made all their family's clothes, and helped in the barns and the fields. When the men in the family left to fight in the war, the women ran the farms, sold crops at market, and took over the management of family businesses.

Whether rich or poor, women helped the armies by providing money, nursing the wounded, and sewing clothes. Some made bullets and others worked as soldiers, messengers, or spies. They were all American heroines and stories of their bravery were found throughout the colonies.

> *We may destroy all the men in America, and we shall still have all we can do to defeat the women.*
>
> —Attributed to British General Lord Cornwallis

The Rise of Independent Women

At the time of the revolution, a married woman had very few rights. Everything she owned belonged to her husband. But the reality of the American Revolution began to change their minds. As women took over the work of the family farm or business, they stopped thinking of things as "his" property. Instead, they began to think of them as "ours."

These independent women stood up for their beliefs, both as Patriots and as Loyalists. In Georgia, Nancy Hart killed a British supporter who confronted her about helping the Patriots. She held others at gunpoint until her husband arrived with help. Deborah Read Franklin took up arms to defend her home against a mob angry over the Stamp Act.

WOMEN SUPPORTED SOLDIERS Women helped the army. When soldiers needed uniforms, women spun cloth from linen or wool. They fed armies using their own crops, but there was often not enough to go around.

Women showed heroism throughout the war. In 1782, Betty Zane helped save Fort Henry in the upper Ohio River Valley. During the battle, she made bullets for the soldiers. When their gunpowder ran out, she ran behind the battle lines to a nearby cabin to find additional supplies. At the cabin, she poured more gunpowder into a tablecloth, and raced back to the fort with it.

Betty Zane made bullets to help the soldiers at Fort Henry. When the gunpowder ran out, she ran to a nearby cabin to get some more.

1778

August
Loyalist female spy warns the British about Americans at Newport; the British send more troops

1780

May
General Washington reports army shortages to Congress

June 3
British plunder Eliza Yonge Wilkinson's sister's plantation near Charleston

June 21
The Sentiments of an American Woman appears in Philadelphia

July
Pennsylvania women raise $300,000 for the Continental Army

1781

July
Emily Geiger carries message, forcing a British retreat

1782

September
Betty Zane helps save Fort Henry from British attack

1787

Young Ladies Academy opens in Philadelphia

1790

New Jersey allows women property owners to vote

WOMEN ATTACKED Some women fled as the opposing army approached. Some took a stand against their attackers. Before the Battle of Saratoga in 1777, a local woman named Jane McCrea stayed behind to meet up with her British soldier **fiancé**. Native Americans working with the British mistook her for a Patriot, and murdered and scalped her. Throughout the war, women on both sides were victims of attacks, beatings, and robberies.

Night of Terror

Eliza Yonge Wilkinson was the daughter of a planter. As a young widow, she lived with her elderly father near Charleston, South Carolina. Following the May surrender of Charleston, Wilkinson went to her sister's nearby plantation. She thought she would be safer there. On June 3, 1780, the house was attacked and robbed by British soldiers. Eliza was lucky. In a letter to her friend, she described how she survived the experience. Although the British did not destroy that plantation, they did destroy many others nearby.

"... They then began to plunder the house of every thing they thought valuable or worth taking. Our trunks were split to pieces, and each mean, pitiful wretch [evil person] cram'd his bosom with the Contents, which were our apparel, &c.

> *O! the king's People are coming. It must be them, for they're all in red.*
>
> —Girl to Eliza Wilkinson, June 3, 1780

"I ventured [tried] to speak to the inhuman monster who had my Clothes. I represented to [told] him the times were such we could not replace what they'd taken from us and beg'd him to spare me only a suit or two, but I got nothing but a hearty curse for my pains. Nay, so far was his callous [unfeeling] heart from relenting [giving up] that, casting his eyes towards my shoes, 'I want them buckles,' said he, and immediately knelt at my feet to take them out. .... The other wretches were employ'd in the same manner. They took my Sister's earrings from her ears, hers and Miss Samuells's buckle. They demanded her ring from her finger; she pleaded for it, told them it was her wedding ring and beg'd they'd let her keep it; but they still demanded it, and presenting a Pistol at her, swore if she did not deliver it immediately, they'd fire. She gave it to them; and after bundling up all their Booty, they mounted their horses. ....

"They took care to tell us when they were going away that they had favor'd us a great deal—that we might thank our Stars it was no worse."

—*Eliza Yonge Wilkinson*

Female Soldiers and Spies

Both the British and Continental armies had female supporters. Some women even travelled with the armies. Women could not officially enlist as soldiers. Instead, they did laundry, cooked meals, and nursed the wounded.

Many of these women were following their husbands. Poor families could not afford to have a man away from home. Such families were better off with the army, where they were usually fed. In these cases, the entire family went on the march.

Women and children were issued rations but received less food than the men. They were also supposed to stay at the back of the army when it was on the march. General Washington sometimes got impatient with the "multitude of women" with his army. But he recognized the importance of feeding them or risk losing "by Desertion, perhaps to the Enemy, some of the oldest and best Soldiers In the Service."

> " [T]he british [sic] Prisoners of War . . . have Herds of Women with them.
>
> —Robert Morris, Patriot financier, February 1783 "

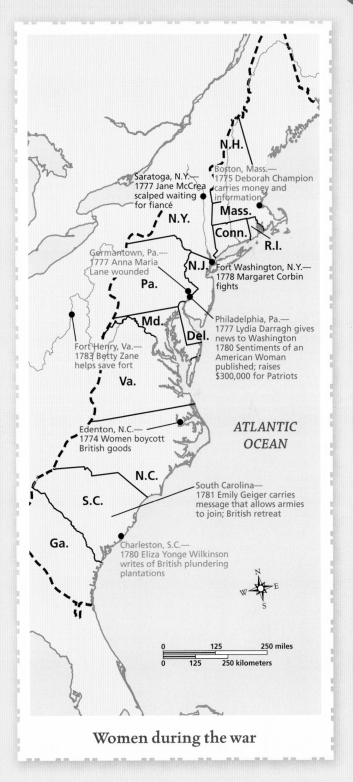

Women during the war

Deborah Champion, Female Courier

During the war, many ordinary people carried out brave deeds. Although Deborah Champion was not part of the army, she helped the Patriot cause. She was the daughter of Colonel Champion, one of three men in charge of supplying money and materials to the Patriot forces. The family lived in Connecticut.

In 1775, Deborah Champion carried money and information through British lines to Boston. She was able to avoid suspicion from British soldiers because they thought she was an old woman in her cloak and bonnet. Champion was able to deliver a hundred dollars in colonial bills to George Washington and return home safely.

> "
> *Well, here I am home again safe and sound and happy to have been of use.*
> —Deborah Champion, 1775
> "

Lydia Darragh, Quaker Spy

Living near the enemy, women could often keep an eye on troop movements and pass this information on to the Patriots. Lydia Darragh was a Quaker woman who supported the war effort. This is uncommon for Quakers, whose religious beliefs reject war. When the British occupied Philadelphia, they took over the Darragh home. Since Lydia Darragh had nowhere else to go, she was allowed to stay.

Lydia Darragh lived on Second Street in Philadelphia when the British took over her home. She listened in on conversations and passed information on to the Patriots.

On December 2, the British used her home to plan an attack on Washington's forces nearby. Listening from a linen closet, Darragh collected details of the attack. The next day she asked permission to go out to get flour, but she really went to alert Washington's army. He heard of the planned attack in time to prepare a defense.

Ann Bates, Loyalist Spy

Other women served as spies. Ann Bates was a Philadelphia schoolteacher who spied for the British. Bates was married to a man who joined the British army. She disguised herself as a **peddler**. She could then listen in on conversations and observe gun placements. In 1778, information from Ann convinced the British to send more men to Rhode Island. This action caused the French and Patriots to withdraw from Rhode Island.

Margaret Arnold, Turncoat Patriot

Some people appeared to be Patriots, but were actually helping the British. One of these was Margaret, the wife of Benedict Arnold. Benedict Arnold collected secret information he passed on to the British. When her husband was arrested, Margaret Arnold claimed that she knew nothing about his work, but she had in fact been helping him.

> *I have only one question, . . . what did you do with the letter?*
> *Emily: I ate it!*
> —General Sumter

After the war, Margaret lived in Britain, where she received a **pension** for her service to the government. If the war had ended differently, she would have been considered a heroine.

Emily Geiger, Teen Spy

Sometimes, the information carried by women made the difference between victory and defeat. In 1781, Patriot General Greene was trying to capture a British fort in South Carolina and needed to get a message to General Sumter, who was 70 miles (110 km)

> *One thing is certain the enemy had notice of our coming. . . . The walls must have ears.*
> —British Major André, December 9, 1777

away. If the two generals joined forces, they could defeat the British.

Emily Geiger, the daughter of a wealthy farmer, volunteered to take a message to General Greene. But she was overheard by a British spy, who followed her. Geiger was caught and taken to the British commander. She was locked in a guardhouse while the British decided what to do. They found no evidence of a message, and Geiger was allowed to continue on her way. Geiger eventually caught up with General Sumter and gave him the message even though she was tired and hungry. Sumter's forces joined with those of General Greene, and the British retreated.

Women Soldiers

Some women disguised themselves as men in order to join the army. This was fairly easy. There were no medical examinations back then. Soldiers needed front teeth and a thumb and forefinger in order to load a musket. A woman dressed and acting like a man could pass. Other women became soldiers by chance. Women who were not soldiers helped the men during battle. These women sometimes stepped into the place of an injured soldier.

What Do You Think?

How were women who fought as soldiers able to get away with their disguises? What does that tell you about the level of care for the wounded during the American Revolution?

A Soldier Named Robert

Deborah Sampson worked as a servant from a young age. When the war came, she wanted to fight. In secret, she made a set of men's clothes. She wrapped tight bandages around her breasts to flatten them. Dressed like this, she joined the army as Robert Shurtleff.

Deborah Sampson is revered as a veteran of the American Revolution.

As Robert, Sampson became a general's aide. She served his meals and performed other services. When she was wounded in the head and leg, she let a doctor treat her head injury, but she removed the leg bullet by herself. This protected her secret, although her leg never healed properly. Sampson got a severe fever and was put in the hospital. There a doctor learned her secret when he unwound her bandages. He did not betray her. Instead, he took care of her until she was well. Then he gave "Robert" a letter and sent her to see General Washington.

General Washington gave Sampson an **honorable discharge** and enough money to start a new life. She married a farmer, had three children, and became a schoolteacher. She later gave talks on the war and her part in it. Sometimes, she dressed up in her uniform to show what she looked like as a soldier. In 1792 Deborah Sampson was given a small piece of land and a pension for her military service.

Margaret Corbin, Female Hero

Margaret Corbin followed her husband when he joined the Patriot army. In 1776, her husband was killed at Fort Washington in New York, so she took over loading and firing his cannon. She was wounded by **grapeshot**. When Fort Washington was captured, a doctor helped Corbin. She survived her injuries, but never regained use of her left arm.

In 1779, Margaret was the first woman to receive a pension as a disabled soldier. She got half the pay and allowances of a soldier. The Daughters of the American Revolution reburied her remains at West Point in 1926.

Anna Maria Lane, War Veteran

Little is known about Anna Maria Lane. She and her husband fought in New Jersey, Pennsylvania, and Georgia. Dressed as a man, she was wounded during the Battle of Germantown in 1777. After the war, she worked as a nurse for the Public Guard. The wound continued to bother her. In 1806, the Virginia General Assembly on the recommendation of the governor, granted Lane a pension for her extraordinary war service. She received more than twice the $40 most men got at that time, as **compensation** for her war injury.

> *She fought "with the courage of a soldier."*
>
> —1808 papers giving a pension to Anna Maria Lane

People at the Time
Molly Pitcher

Molly Pitcher fought at the Battle of Monmouth. She took her husband's position after he was injured. Her story became so famous that Molly Pitcher is the nickname for all women who fought during the American Revolution. Like Margaret Corbin and Anna Maria Lane, the names of these women have been lost. Through Molly Pitcher, they are remembered for the bravery they showed.

Molly Pitcher loading a cannon at the Battle of Monmouth. She became so famous that her name now means any woman who fought on the Patriot side.

Women Take Political Action

Before the American Revolution, most women did not discuss politics. The war changed this. Women learned to form opinions and to act on them.

Daughters of Liberty

Parliament taxed the cloth that was sold in America. Colonial women refused to buy it. They formed groups called the "Daughters of Liberty" to weave yarn and wool into homespun cloth. Much of the clothing that Patriots wore was made from this material.

In 1774 Patriot women encouraged the Continental Congress to boycott all British imports. Although making substitutes for goods was hard work, they believed that the boycott was an important way to support the war.

The Edenton Tea Party

British newspapers laughed at the Edenton boycott, but they came to respect America's fighting spirit.

In both Britain and the colonies, tea was a very popular beverage which people drank at social gatherings. The 1773 Tea Act gave the British East India Company a monopoly on selling tea in America. When British Parliament closed the Boston Harbor after the Boston Tea Party, women as well as men protested angrily.

In Edenton, North Carolina, a group of women hosted their own tea party. They promised to boycott all British tea and cloth. They would not buy any that arrived after September 10, 1774. Actions like this strengthened the Patriot position. They also showed how strongly women felt about the war.

Raising Money for the Troops

The Continental Army was often short of money. By May 1780, General George Washington reported shortages of rations, clothing, and pay. Without proper food and clothing, his troops were badly nourished, cold, and exhausted.

In June, a handbill addressed to women appeared in Philadelphia. The handbill was likely written by Esther De Berdt Reed, the governor's wife. It inspired women from Pennsylvania to raise funds. By July 4, the women had raised more than $300,000.

Following Pennsylvania's example, women in Maryland, New Jersey, and Virginia also collected money.

Washington asked the women to use the money for shirts. There was enough to purchase linen to make 2,200 shirts. These were handmade by Patriot women. Each shirt included the embroidered name of the woman who sewed it.

Sentiments of an American Woman

This is part of a handbill printed to promote the women's campaign.

"ON the commencement of actual war, the Women of America manifested a firm resolution to contribute as much as could depend on them, to the deliverance of their country. . . .

"[In] so many famous sieges . . . the Women have been seen . . . resigning the ornaments of their apparel, and their fortune, to fill the public treasury. . . .

"Born for liberty, . . . we associate ourselves to the grandeur of those Sovereigns . . . who . . . have broken the chains of slavery, forged by tyrants. . . . It was the Maid of Orleans who drove from the kingdom of France the ancestors of those same British, . . . whom it is necessary that we drive from this Continent.

". . . *This is the offering of the Ladies.* The time is arrived to display the same sentiments which animated us at the beginning of the Revolution, when we renounced the use of teas, . . . when our republican and laborious hands spun the flax, . . . Let us not lose a moment; . . . and you [soldiers], our brave deliverers, . . . receive with a free hand our offering. . .

"By An AMERICAN WOMAN."

Women Talk About Equality

While husbands were away fighting in the war, their wives took care of their property. Many Patriot women considered themselves included in the idea that "all men are created equal."

> *". . . I desire you would Remember the Ladies, and be more generous and favourable to them than your ancestors."*
>
> —Abigail Adams to her husband, John Adams, while he attended the Continental Congress

In 1776, Abigail Adams suggested that her husband talk to the Continental Congress about changing the laws for women. At that time, married women had very few rights. Everything a woman owned—property, money, livestock, buildings, jewelry—belonged to her husband after marriage.

March 31, 1776, Letter from Abigail Adams to Her Husband

"I long to hear that you have declared an independency—and by the way in the new Code of Laws which I suppose it will be necessary for you to make I desire you would Remember the Ladies, and be more generous and favourable to them than your ancestors. Do not put such unlimited power into the hands of the Husbands.

"Remember all Men would be **tyrants** if they could. If particular care and attention is not paid to the Ladies we are determined to **foment** a Rebellion, and will not hold ourselves bound by any Laws in which we have no voice, or representation.

"That your Sex are Naturally Tyrannical is a Truth so thoroughly established as to admit of no dispute, but such of you as wish to be happy willing give up the harsh title of Master for the more tender and endearing one of Friend. Why, then, not put it out of the power of the vicious and the Lawless to use us with cruelty and indignity with impunity. Men of Sense in all Ages abhor those customs which treat us only as the vassals of your Sex. Regard us then as Beings placed by providence under your protection and in imitation of the Supreme Being make use of that power only for our happiness."

Abigail Adams corresponded with and advised her husband, John Adams, during the Continental Congress.

Women in New Jersey Allowed to Vote

According to the 1776 New Jersey constitution, women property owners could vote. A 1790 change read: "No person shall be entitled to vote in any other township or precinct, than that in which he or she doth actually reside." Women property owners voted until 1807, when voting was restricted to "free, white, male citizens of this state."

Girls Go to School

After the war, schools for girls opened up throughout the colonies. There were academies for rich families in Philadelphia, Bethlehem, and Boston that gave girls an education similar to that of boys. Girls from less well-off families could learn basic reading, writing, and sums at home or in community schools. Many of these schools were for boys and girls. But women who completed high school could not go to universities. This did not happen until well into the 1800s.

> " . . . it is by the female world that the greatest and best characters among men are born.
>
> —John Adams to his daughter, Nabby, August 13, 1783

People at the Time

Susanna Rowson

Susanna Rowson worked as a governess in Britain before coming to America in 1793. She authored *Charlotte Temple*, the first American best-selling novel written by a woman. In 1797, she started Mrs. Rowson's Academy for Young Ladies in Boston. The school educated daughters of the middle class. Rowson was director of the school until 1822. During that time, she also wrote poems and school textbooks.

The West Chester Ladies' Seminary in West Chester, Pennsylvania, welcomed female pupils in the late 1700s and early 1800s.

Slaves Fight for Freedom

African-born Americans and their descendants played a significant role in the Revolutionary War for both the Patriots and the Loyalists.

Major Events

1775

April 19
Peter Salem fights at Battle of Concord

June 17
Salem Poor cited for bravery in Battle of Bunker Hill; Peter Salem kills British major

November 7
British offer freedom to black slaves who joined them

November 12
General Washington ends recruitment of black soldiers

1776

Winter
General Washington urges Continental Congress to allow free blacks in the army

Slavery in the Colonies

Both free blacks and slaves were important to the American Revolution. From the first arrival of Africans on slave ships, the black population in the colonies grew steadily. By 1750, black people in the northern and middle colonies comprised more than 15 percent of the regions' population. They represented nearly 25 percent of the population in the Southern colonies. By the start of the war 25 years later, there were slaves in all 13 colonies, with more than half of the black population living in Virginia and Maryland.

Loyalist Black Soldiers

Needing more troops in the fall of 1775, British Lord Dunmore offered freedom to Patriot-owned slaves who were "able and willing to bear arms" for the British. Estimated figures suggest that "Lord Dunmore's Proclamation" attracted 800 to 1,000 escaped slaves. About a third of these were women, even though his proclamation applied only to males. Other British commanders also used the promise of freedom to encourage Patriot-owned slaves to run away. In the South, an estimated 10,000 black slaves ran to British lines.

Those who joined the British navy helped navigate waterways and were allowed to man cannons in ship combat. Very few Loyalist black soldiers, however, were allowed to fight. The British army used black soldiers as drummers and **fifers,** or to dig trenches, build fortifications, repair roads, drive wagons, and perform other duties that freed white soldiers for combat. Some did fight as cavalrymen or risked their lives as spies.

The British didn't follow through on their promise of freedom to all slaves. When they took over some plantations owned by Patriots, British officers often sold their black soldiers to British sugar cane plantation owners in the Caribbean.

Lord Dunmore's 1775 Proclamation

. . . I do in Virtue of the Power and Authority to ME given, by His MAJESTY, determine to execute Martial Law, and cause the same to be executed throughout this Colony: and . . . [so that] Peace and good Order may the sooner be restored, I do require every Person capable of bearing Arms, to resort to His MAJESTY'S STANDARD, or be looked up as Traitors to His MAJESTY'S Crown and Government, and thereby become liable to the Penalty the Law inflicts upon such Offences; such a forfeiture of Life, confiscation of Lands, &. &. And I do hereby further declare all indented Servants, Negroes, and others (appertaining to Rebels,) free that are able and willing to bear Arms, they joining His MAJESTY'S Troops as soon as may be, . . .

LORD DUNMORE'S REGIMENT

Within a month, black people came from long distances to join Lord Dunmore's Ethiopian Regiment. In 1775 to 1776, Lord Dunmore commanded 2,000 men, half of them black. This Ethiopian regiment consisted of black men led by white British officers and sergeants. The fronts of the regiment's uniforms read "Liberty to Slaves." Additional slaves flocked to the British side when British General Cornwallis invaded the Carolinas in 1780 to 1781.

Major Events

1776

February 23
Rhode Island agrees to free slaves who joined the Continental Army

June 28
Titus Tye fights for the British at the Battle of Monmouth

August 29
All-black regiment fights for Patriots in Battle of Rhode Island

1779
Titus Tye leads a troop of Loyalist guerillas called the Black Brigade

1781
British move black Loyalist soldiers to Canada

1780s
Massachusetts abolishes slavery

1792
Black Loyalists found Freetown, in what is now Sierra Leone, West Africa

Slaves as Soldiers: A Difficult Idea

Africans and African Americans were looked down upon and considered to be useful only for manual labor because of the existence of slavery. Especially in the Southern colonies—where blacks outnumbered whites by nearly two to one—white masters depended on slave labor to run their farms and plantations. They could not afford to let their slaves go off to fight in the war and feared a slave rebellion if slaves were allowed to be armed.

Many Patriot leaders urged having black men—both free blacks and slaves—as soldiers due to the loss of manpower during the war. Many thought that slaves could be prevented from going to the British if they were set free and encouraged to enlist in the Patriot army.

Patriots Recruit Slaves

During the winter of 1777–1778, prospects for the Patriots looked bleak. The British occupied major cities. Supplies and **morale** were low. The Patriot army continued to shrink. Colonies were having problems raising the soldier **quotas** set by Congress in 1776.

RHODE ISLAND In Rhode Island, it seemed that the only way to meet quotas was to recruit slaves. By February 23, 1778, the Rhode Island General Assembly **decreed** that individual slaves who joined the army would be freed from slavery. White soldiers agreed to fight for only 90 days. Black, mixed-race, and Native American soldiers had to fight for the entire war to gain their freedom. Approximately 250 men joined the army. This group became part of the First Rhode Island Regiment.

SOUTHERN PLANTATIONS The Continental Congress also took action on the slave issue to address Southern plantation owners. It decreed that slaves needed permission from their masters. When a slave was admitted, he became a free man, and his master was compensated with money from the colony, depending on the slave's value.

What Do You Know!

FIRST RHODE ISLAND REGIMENT

The First Rhode Island Regiment included black, **mulatto**, and a few Narragansett Native American soldiers led by white officers. This regiment protected Washington's army as they retreated from Newport in August 1778. Soldiers in the regiment wore white uniforms with brown sashes and tall plumed blue hats. They stood out, which made it easier for the British to target them. Despite repeated attacks, the soldiers held fast for most of the day.

Black Patriot Soldiers

At least 5,000 black soldiers fought for the Patriots in the Continental Army. They fought at almost every action, including the Battles of Lexington and Concord, Bunker Hill, Valley Forge, and Saratoga. Black sailors helped as able seamen and pilots.

One eyewitness account gives an idea of the number of black soldiers in the Continental Army in a 1777 army report: "[N]o regiment is to be seen in which there are not Negroes in abundance; and among them there are able bodied, strong and brave fellows."

Salem Poor

Salem Poor was a Massachusetts slave who bought his freedom in 1769. He enlisted with the Patriots in 1775. In the Battle of Bunker Hill, Salem mortally wounded a British lieutenant colonel. Fourteen officers commended his bravery, reporting "We declare that A Negro Man Called Salem Poor . . . behaved like an Experienced Officer, as Well as an Excellent Soldier, . . . We . . . beg leave to say in the Person of this Negro Centers a Brave & gallant Soldier."

Salem continued to serve with Patriot forces until 1780.

This painting by John Singleton Copley shows the 1781 death of Major Pierson in the Battle of Jersey. On the left, Pierson's black servant, Pompey, takes revenge on the person who shot Pierson.

Thomas Peters was born in Nigeria. He was captured and sold by slave traders in 1760. Peters constantly tried to run away from his masters and was sold to several different owners. In 1776, he fled from his master's North Carolina flour mill. He joined the Black Pioneers, a Loyalist regiment made up of runaway slaves. Peters showed a great deal of leadership and later became a sergeant.

Runaway Slaves Join British

Titus Tye, also known as Colonel Tye, was an African slave in New Jersey. His owner was known to be especially cruel. When the British offered freedom to slaves that would join the royal forces, Tye—along with 300 other escaped slaves—fled to join the British troops in Norfolk, Virginia. The newspaper ad below advertises for his return.

> *THREE POUNDS Reward.*
> Run away from the subscriber, living in Shrewsbury, in the county of Monmouth, New Jersey, a NEGROE man, named Titus, but may probably change his name; he is about 21 years of age, not very black, near 6 feet high; had on a grey homespun coat, brown breeches, blue and white stockings, and took with him a wallet, drawn up at one end with a string, in which was a quantity of clothes. Whoever takes up said Negroe, and secures him in any goal [jail], or brings him to me, shall be entitled to the above reward or Three Pounds proc. and all reasonable charges, paid by
> *Nov 8, 1775.*   *JOHN CORLIS*

Tye quickly earned British officers' respect and was promoted to commander of the Black Brigade. After fighting at the Battle of Monmouth, he and a band of **guerillas** raided homes in New Jersey. They attacked their former masters and robbed Patriot homes, killing many Patriot leaders. In 1779, Tye helped British troops free many slaves. However, he died in 1780 at the age of 27 from a musket wound.

> "
> *We hear a declaration his Lordship [Lord Dunmore] has made, of proclaiming all the Negroes free, who should join him, has startled the insurgents [Patriots.]*
>
> —General Thomas Gage
>

Washington Changes Mind About Black Soldiers

General Washington was hesitant about allowing black soldiers in his army. Many of the Patriots depended on slave labor. They worried that slaves who knew how to handle and shoot guns might turn against their Patriot masters.

On November 12, 1775, Washington issued orders **prohibiting** black men from serving in the Continental Army. This included both slaves and free blacks. Washington reversed his order by the winter of 1776. Fearing that the blacks might join the British, he then encouraged enlisting free blacks.

Ned Griffin Petitions for Freedom

Some colonists supported the Patriots but did not want to join the Continental Army. Such colonists could purchase a slave to serve in the army for them. These slaves were often promised their freedom in return for military service.

William Kitchen of North Carolina purchased a slave named Ned Griffin as his substitute. Later, Kitchen refused to keep his promise. Griffin petitioned the North Carolina legislature. He won both his freedom and the right to vote. Freedom petitions like Griffin's were common during the Revolution. Many were granted.

🌠 What Do You Know!

HAITIAN SOLDIERS
After General Washington lifted the ban on African American soldiers in the Continental Army, some 500 black soldiers came from Haiti in the Caribbean to help the Patriots in Savannah, Georgia. They were the single largest unit of soldiers fighting against the British in Savannah.

This statue in Savannah, Georgia, remembers the Haitian soldiers who served with the Continental Army.

> *This dreadful rumour [about re-enslavement] filled us with inexpressible anguish and terror, especially when we saw our old masters, coming from Virginia, North-Carolina and other parts, and seizing upon their slaves in the streets of New-York, or even dragging them out of their beds.*
>
> —Boston King, black Baptist preacher, 1782

What Happened After the War?

After the war, some slaves were reclaimed by their owners. Others left America with other Loyalists. Some black Loyalists went to Britain or Nova Scotia in Canada. Others went to East Florida or to Sierra Leone in Africa.

Many black Patriots also won their freedom. Lieutenant Olney, who had led the First Rhode Island battalion, helped many veterans get the pensions and past wages owed to them.

Black slave women were not as fortunate. They could not win their freedom because they could not fight with the army. The fortunate ones had masters who fed them well, did not mistreat them, and possibly even educated them. The less fortunate had to deal with cruelty from abusive masters. Slave women in the North were more fortunate than those in the South. Starting with Massachusetts in the 1780s, many Northern states outlawed slavery.

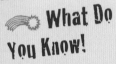

What Do You Know!

After the war, Thomas Peters went to Nova Scotia. He later convinced over 1,100 black Loyalists to follow him to Sierra Leone. In 1792, they founded Freetown on the west coast of Africa.

> *Tell them that if I am Black I am free born American & a revolutionary soldier & therefore ought not to be entirely out of the scale of notice.*
>
> —John Chavis, black former soldier in Fifth Virginia Regiment, 1832

America After the War

T he Revolutionary War secured independence for the United States of America. But the new country had to rebuild its economy after the war.

Continental Dollar Drops

In 1781, after six years of fighting, the economy was in a mess. The war started as a dispute over taxes. During the war, Continental Congress needed money to pay for the fight. Congress could not collect taxes under the first constitution, the Articles of Confederation. They borrowed money from France but it was not enough.

In order to pay for the war, Continental Congress issued paper money in 1775. Paper money is a form of **credit**. It promises that the people who print the money will pay the value on the bill.

The Continental Congress printed $250 million in paper bills. This was more money than they had. By 1781, everyone knew this. The continental dollar was worthless. The value of the dollar made it difficult for soldiers who had been paid with these bills. It also caused problems for people who had accepted the bills. They were not worth the goods they sold in exchange.

Major Events

1775
Continental Congress issues paper money

1776
British **blockade** Atlantic coast

1777
March Delegates from several states agree on price and wage controls

1781
Continental dollar is worthless

September French fleet blockades Yorktown for the Patriots

1780s
States pass laws to help farmers deal with war debt

The continental paper dollar was first printed in 1775. By 1781, the paper dollar was considered worthless.

39

Blockade Stops Trade

At the time of the American Revolution, there were few roads within the colonies. Goods were transported on rivers or on the Atlantic Ocean.

The British blockaded the Atlantic Coast during most of the war. This affected trade among the colonies and with other countries. Before the war, colonist merchants made a lot of money in what is called a "trading triangle." Textiles, rum, and manufactured goods from Europe were traded down the coast of Africa for black slaves. These slaves were taken to the colonies. In exchange, the colonists sent sugar and tobacco to Europe.

What Do You Think?

How did the British blockade disrupt the trading triangle?

Blockade Causes Unemployment

Before the war, colonists grew enough food for themselves, and also exported about one-fifth of their grain crop. The British blockade stopped this trade. The British blockade also caused unemployment. Everyone who worked on the ships or unloaded and sold goods was affected. Wealthy people who depended on trade had a hard time making ends meet. Some lost everything. Poor people were much worse off. Some followed the armies because they had no other place to go. With the army, they might at least get fed.

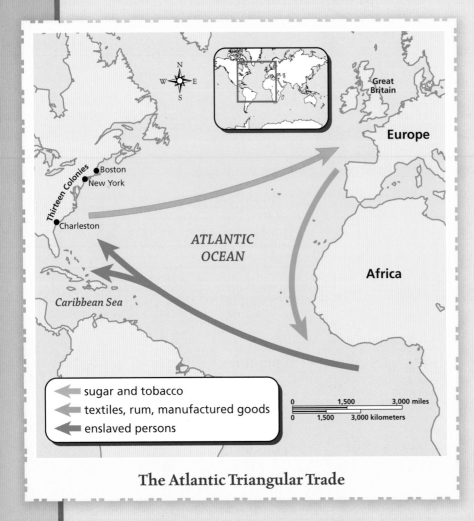

The Atlantic Triangular Trade

sugar and tobacco

textiles, rum, manufactured goods

enslaved persons

Economy Slows

Wars can sometimes help an economy because armies use a lot of goods. Wars need soldiers to fight. Soldiers need to be fed, clothed, and housed.

During the Revolution, colonists worked hard to fulfill the army's needs. In some ways, this was good for the economy. It meant that people were busy supplying goods and services needed for the army. On the other hand, items became scarce. Prices went up because there was not enough to go around.

During the war, much of the money paid to workers was worthless. People did not want to take the money for debts or goods.

Taking Advantage of Shortages

There were people who took advantage of the situation. While the Continental Army starved at Valley Forge, some farmers got high prices for food they sold to the British army. Colonists tried to prevent such food shortages by agreeing to wage and price controls.

Food shortages and **inflation** continued after the war. British goods flooded the market, competing with more expensive American items. There were restrictions on exports to Britain. This reduced trade. Many farmers were in debt and losing their land. During the 1780s, the new states passed laws to help farmers deal with their debt. People who had loaned money to the farmers were unhappy. But it was a way of improving the economy.

Worthwhile Homefront Sacrifices

Life in colonial America was not easy. Families and communities worked hard to feed, house, and clothe themselves. Fighting a war for independence made life even harder, as many men left to fight. However, for the Patriots, the sacrifices were well worth the hardship. In the war and on the homefront, together Americans won their independence and the United States of America was born.

What Do You Know!

PAPER MONEY
In some colonies, it was against the law to refuse continental dollars. Punishments included fines, imprisonment, and loss of the property concerned.

GLOSSARY

acquit to determine innocent of a crime

ban to outlaw use or possession of something

blockade a military tactic in which enemy ships keep goods from coming in or going out of a port

boycott to refuse to buy, often for a political purpose

card combing with a card to remove fibers or seeds; the step before spinning in wool processing

compensation payment for a service

confiscate to take away

cooper an artisan who makes barrels

credit a promise of future payment

customs the office or officials who collect import or export taxes

dame school a small village school run by a woman in her home

decree to pronounce or proclaim; to say publicly

economy the exchange of goods, services, and money

fiancé the person another person intends to marry

fifer one who plays the fife, a small flute

financier banker or other financial professional

foment to start or inspire

frontier the edge of the settled world

game wild animals that are hunted for food or sport

good a product or manufactured item

grammar school elementary school

grapeshot small balls (approximately ½–1 in or 2–3 cm) made of lead or iron shot from a cannon

guerrilla a soldier fighting in a surprise or non-traditional setting; often fighters are not part of a formal military unit

honorable discharge the designation given to soldiers who have completed their service with honor

indentured servant a servant bound to serve for a certain term of time, often in exchange for immigration passage

inflation increase in the price of goods; decrease in the buying power of money

linsey-woolsey a coarse fabric made from cross-weaved linen and wool

Loyalist one who sided with Great Britain in the Revolutionary War, wanted the colonies to remain in the British Empire

merchant someone who buys or sells goods for profit

midwife one who helps women give birth, often a trained female elder of the village

migrate to move permanently to a new place, often a new country

monopoly the economic condition under which a single company has control over the whole market of one good

morale the overall feeling of citizens or an army about accomplishing a task

mulatto of mixed race parentage, often with one white parent and one black parent

occupying army an army who takes over an area; often the civilians in the area were or are in support of the opposing army

Parliament the British government; made up of the House of Lords and the House of Commons and headed by the prime minister

patriotism a feeling of loyalty to one's nation or country

Patriot one who desired independence for the American colonies from Great Britain

peddler one who travels to sell goods, often with a wagon or cart

pension a living stipend or sum of money given monthly or yearly after a person retires from an organization

plantation a large estate supported by agriculture; in the colonies often supported by slave labor

prohibit to outlaw or prevent from doing

prosper to thrive or do well

prosperity success or doing well

quota a goal number or limit number of

repeal to cancel a law

revenue funds brought in, often to pay for government or other spending

seize to take, generally without permission

slave a person made to work without compensation

statesman a skilful politician; a political figure who works for the good of the community or nation

traitor one who betrays his or her country

tyrant a ruler who has all the power; a ruler who uses power cruelly over others

TIMELINE

1607–1732		The 13 American colonies are founded
1754–1763		Great Britain defeats France in the French and Indian War
1764	*April*	Parliament passes the Sugar Act
1765	*March 22*	Parliament passes the Stamp Act
	March 24	Parliament passes the Quartering Act
1766	*March*	Parliament repeals the Stamp Act but passes the Declaratory Act
1767	*June 29*	Parliament passes the Townshend Revenue Act
1770	*March 5*	The Boston Massacre
1773	*May 10*	Parliament passes the Tea Act
	December 16	The Boston Tea Party
1774	*March*	Parliament passes the Intolerable Acts
	September 5	Patriots meet for the First Continental Congress
1775	*April 19*	American Revolution begins with the Battle of Lexington
	November 7	British offers freedom to black slaves
	November 12	General Washington ends recruitment of black soldiers
1780	*May*	General Washington reports army shortages to Continental Congress
1780s		Massachusetts abolishes slavery
1781		British move black Loyalist soldiers to Canada
1783	*September 3*	The Treaty of Paris is signed, officially ending the war

FURTHER READING AND WEBSITES

Books

Aloian, Molly. *George Washington: Hero of the American Revolution.* Crabtree Publishing Company, 2013.

Aloian, Molly. *Phillis Wheatley: Poet of the Revolutionary Era.* Crabtree Publishing Company, 2013.

Clarke, Gordon. *Significant Battles of the American Revolution.* Crabtree Publishing Company, 2013.

Cocca, Lisa Colozza. *Marquis de Lafayette: Fighting for America's Freedom.* Crabtree Publishing Company, 2013.

Kalman, Bobbie. *Colonial Life.* Crabtree Publishing Company, 1992

Kalman, Bobbie and Bishop, Amanda. *A Slave Family.* Crabtree Publishing Company, 2003

Perritano, John. The *Causes of the American Revolution.* Crabtree Publishing Company, 2013.

Perritano, John. The *Outcome of the American Revolution.* Crabtree Publishing Company, 2013.

Rinaldi, Ann. *Hang a Thousand Trees with Ribbons: The Story of Phillis Wheatley.* Gulliver Books, 1996

Roberts, Steve. *King George III: England's Struggle to Keep America.* Crabtree Publishing Company, 2013.

Websites

"Boston Tea Party Historical Society." **www.boston-tea-party.org/ smuggling/John-Hancock.html**

"Colonial Williamsburg." **www.history.org/Almanack/life/ index.cfm**

"National Archives." **www.archives.gov/education/ lessons/revolution-images/**

"National Park Service." **www.nps.gov/vafo/historyculture/ upload/Philadelphia%20Campaign.pdf**

"North Carolina Museum of History." **www.ncmuseumofhistory.org/ collateral/articles/F92.libertytoslaves.pdf**

"Oracle ThinkQuest." **http://library.thinkquest.org/TQ0312848/ dsampson.htm**

"Social Studies for Kids." **www.socialstudiesforkids.com/ articles/ushistory/13coloniesfarm.htm**

"U.S. Department of State: Office of the Historian." **http://history.state.gov/milestones/ 1750-1775/ParliamentaryTaxation**

BIBLIOGRAPHY

Books

Kalman, Bobbie. *Colonial Life*. Crabtree Publishing Company, 1992.

Kalman, Bobbie and Bishop, Amanda. *A Slave Family*. Crabtree Publishing Company, 2003.

Lehman, David, ed. *The Oxford Book of American Poetry*. Oxford University Press, 2006.

Parkinson, Roger. *The American Revolution*. London: Wayland Publishers, 1971.

Rinaldi, Ann. *Hang a Thousand Trees with Ribbons: The Story of Phillis Wheatley*. Gulliver Books, 1996.

Roberts, Cokie. *Founding Mothers: The Women Who Raised Our Nation*. HarperCollins, 2004.

Speare, Elizabeth George. *Life in Colonial America*. Randon House, Inc., 1963.

Websites

"AmericanRevolution.org"
http://www.americanrevolution.org/women/women20.html

"Boston Tea Party Historical Society"
http://www.boston-tea-party.org/timeline.html

"Colonel Tye (1753–1780)"
http://www.blackpast.org/?q=aah/colonel-tye-1753-1780

"Connecticut Historical Society"
http://emuseum.chs.org:8080/emuseum/view/people/asitem/items$0040nul7

"HistoryCentral.com"
http://www.historycentral.com/NN/Americans/Women.html

"Library of Congress"
http://www.loc.gov

"Massachusetts Historical Society"
http://www.masshist.org/digitaladams/aea/letter/index.html

"National Archives"
http://www.archives.gov/education/lessons/revolution-images/

"National Humanities Center"
http://nationalhumanitiescenter.org/pds/makingrev/war/text7/reedsentimentsamerwoman.pdf

"National Park Service"
http://www.nps.gov/vafo/historyculture/upload/Philadelphia%20Campaign.pdf

"North Carolina History Project"
http://www.northcarolinahistory.org/commentary/50/entry

"North Carolina Museum of History"
http://www.ncmuseumofhistory.org/collateral/articles/F92.libertytoslaves.pdf

"SCORE"
http://score.rims.k12.ca.us/score_lessons/women_american_revolution/corbin.html

"Teach American History"
http://www.teachamericanhistory.org/File/Margaret_Corbin_Molly_Pitcher.pdf

"Women in the U.S. Army"
http://www.army.mil/women/history.html

INDEX

Index